BASKETBALL LEGENDS ALPHABET

Words by Robin Feiner

Aa

A is for Kareem Abdul-Jabbar. As the all-time leader in points scored and career wins, 'The Captain' is the greatest center of all time. This colossal legend was even awarded the Presidential Medal of Freedom.

B is for Larry Bird.
Playing his entire career
for the Boston Celtics,
'Larry Legend' is the only
person in history to be
named Rookie of the Year,
Regular Season MVP, Finals
MVP, All-Star MVP, Coach
of the Year and Executive
of the Year.

C is for Stephen Curry. The 'Baby-Faced Assassin' started shooting hoops at the age of only five. As the NBA's deadliest shooter, he holds the record for the most three-pointers in a season in both the NBA and NCAA.

D is for **D**avid Robinson. Playing for the San Antonio Spurs his entire career, 'The Admiral' was Sports Illustrated Magazine's Sportsman of the Year in 2003. He's a 10-time NBA All-Star and considered one of the game's most legendary centers.

E is for Julius Erving. With a flair for scoring, spins and dramatic jump shots, he landed two ABA championships, an NBA championship and 11 NBA All-Star appearances. 'Doctor J's' legendary dunks and graceful play helped change the game.

F is for Walt Frazier. This dazzling player with hands "faster than a lizard's tongue," was known for his flamboyant style. Walt 'Clyde' Frazier left the Knicks after 10 years, holding team records for points scored, games played and assists.

G is for Kevin **G**arnett. Measuring an impressive 6'11", this larger-than-life character is the youngest in NBA history to play 1000 games. 'The Big Ticket' is tied for third-most All-Star selections in NBA history. Legend!

H is for **H**akeem Olajuwon. Nicknamed 'The Dream,' this giant of a man led the Houston Rockets to the championships with formidable scoring, rebounding and shot-blocking. He is celebrated as one of the 50 Greatest Players in NBA history.

I is for Allen Iverson. Known to fans as 'The Answer,' this NBA legend was one of the most astounding scorers in the history of the game. In his 14-year career he was a four-time NBA scoring champion and 11-time NBA All-Star.

J is for Michael Jordan. 'Air Jordan' dazzled crowds with his prolific scoring, incredible defense and famous gravity-defying slam dunks. He is without question the greatest of all time, possessing enough star power to globalize the sport.

K is for **K**obe Bryant. Playing his entire 20-year career with the Los Angeles Lakers, this gigantic legend of the game sits third on the NBA all-time scoring list. 'Black Mamba' also proudly boasts two Olympic gold medals.

L is for **L**eBron James. This 'free agent' doesn't like to sit still, but is now formally signed to the Los Angeles Lakers. LeBron is called 'The King' for a reason ... he's considered the best active player in the game and one of the greatest of all time.

M is for Earvin 'Magic' Johnson. The only player in history to win the NBA Finals Most Valuable Player Award in his rookie season, he was known for mesmerizing opponents with breathtaking ability, and then crushing them with his killer instinct.

N is for Dirk Nowitzki. The 'Bavarian Bomber' was a pioneer on the court. This legend is the Mavericks' all-time leader in points, games and minutes played. In 2006, he became the tallest player to win the Three-Point Contest at All-Star Weekend.

O is for **O**scar Robertson. One for the archives, this b-ball legend was the first black player in the history of the University of Cincinnati. 'The Big O' was the first player to average a triple-double over an entire season, a record that stood for 55 seasons!

P is for **P**hil Jackson. Revolutionizing the game with his holistic coaching style, he won a legendary 11 championship titles – six with the Bulls and five with the Lakers, making this 'Zen master' the only coach to win multiple championships with more than one team!

Q is for Shaquille O'Neal. Possibly the most dominant man in the history of the NBA, 'Shaq Daddy' was known for his muscle, aggression and dunks. This giant points scorer earned himself entry into both the Naismith and FIBA Halls of Fame.

R is for Bill **R**ussell.
With majestic defense,
he helped reimagine how
basketball should be played.
'Russ' earned five MVPs,
played in 12 All-Star games,
and won a record 11 NBA
championships. No wonder
he was once named the
'Greatest Player in the
History of the NBA.'

S is for **S**cottie Pippen. This 'Dream Team' member had a legendary 17-year career, playing 12 of those with the Bulls. He is the only player to have won an NBA title and Olympic gold medal in the same year, twice. Boom!

T is for **T**im Duncan. The five-time NBA champion spent 19 years with the San Antonio Spurs and earned himself a reputation as the greatest power forward of all time. 'The Big Fundamental' is probably the greatest Spurs player ever.

U is for Wes Unseld.
This Naismith Hall of Famer
spent his entire career with
the Washington Bullets as
a player, coach and finally,
general manager. He is
one of just two players in
NBA history to win Rookie
of the Year and Most
Valuable Player in the very
same season.

V is for **V**ince Carter. One of the greatest dunkers of all-time, 'Vinsanity' electrified the 2000 Slam Dunk Contest with a series of jaw-dropping slams. Shaquille O'Neal famously called this legend "half man, half amazing."

W is for Wilt Chamberlain. At a towering 7'1", 'Wilt the Stilt' is a legend of the game with several legendary records, including most points scored in one season and being the only player to score 100 points in a single game.

X is for Clyde Drexler. Nicknamed 'The Glide,' he was known for his high-flying, yet seemingly effortless swoops to the basket. During his daring career, he was a 10-time All-Star and named one of the 50 Greatest Players in NBA History.

Y is for **Y**ao Ming.
At a mammoth 7'6" this
Chinese basketballer,
who played his NBA career
with the Houston Rockets,
is the tallest player ever
inducted into the Hall of
Fame. He had the honor
of representing his home
country at three consecutive
Olympic Games.

Zz

Z is for **Z**elmo Beaty.
In an era of big centers,
'Big Z' dominated his
position. The two-time NBA
All-Star made the move to
the ABA, where he helped
the Utah Stars win the 1971
championship. Strength,
determination and integrity:
remember Zelmo Beaty.

The ever-expanding legendary library

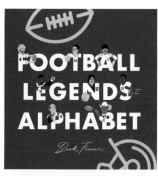

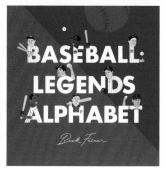

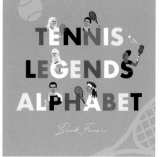

EXPLORE THESE LEGENDARY ALPHABETS & MORE AT WWW.ALPHABETLEGENDS.COM

BASKETBALL LEGENDS ALPHABET
www.alphabetlegends.com

Published by Alphabet Legends Pty Ltd in 2019
Created by Beck Feiner
Copyright © Alphabet Legends Pty Ltd 2019

9780648261667